Harrods
KNIGHTSBRIDGE
ENTERTAINING
Book

Harrods
KNIGHTSBRIDGE
ENTERTAINING
Book

ᘒ

EBURY PRESS STATIONERY

First published in 1992 by Ebury Press Stationery
An imprint of the Random Century Group
Random Century House, 20 Vauxhall Bridge Road,
London SW1V 2SA
Copyright © Random Century Group 1992

Also available: Harrods Wedding Guest Book
Harrods Wedding Planner Book

Set in Shelly Script
by 🅰 Tek Art Ltd., Addiscombe, Croydon, Surrey

Printed in Italy

Designed by Polly Dawes

ISBN 0 09175 126 8

Cover illustration: *The Corner of the
Table,* Paul Chabas (1869-1937)
Back cover illustration: *An Elegant Tea Party in the Artist's Studio,*
Madeleine Lemaire (1845-1928)

Occasion

DATE

TIME

PLACE

TYPE OF PARTY

NUMBER OF GUESTS

Menu

FOOD

_____

_____

_____

_____

_____

_____

_____

COST

_____

_____

_____

WINE

_____

_____

_____

_____

_____

_____

_____

COST

_____

_____

_____

Guests

Comments

_____

_____

_____

_____

_____

_____

_____

_____

_____

_____

_____

Occasion

_____

DATE _____

TIME _____

PLACE _____

_____

_____

TYPE OF PARTY _____

_____

NUMBER OF GUESTS _____

_____

_____

Menu

FOOD

WINE

_____

_____

_____

_____

_____

_____

_____

COST

_____

_____

Guests

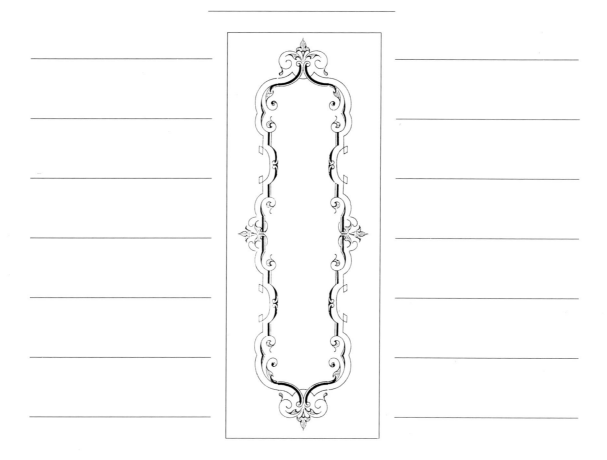

_____

_____

_____

_____

_____

_____

_____

_____

_____

_____

_____

_____

_____

Comments

_____

_____

_____

_____

_____

_____

_____

_____

_____

_____

_____

_____

Occasion

DATE

TIME

PLACE

TYPE OF PARTY

NUMBER OF GUESTS

Menu

FOOD

WINE

_____

_____

_____

_____

_____

_____

_____

COST

_____

_____

_____

Guests

_____

_____   _____

_____   _____

_____   _____

_____   _____

_____   _____

_____   _____

_____

Comments

_____

_____

_____

_____

_____

_____

_____

_____

_____

_____

_____

_____

Occasion

DATE

TIME

PLACE

TYPE OF PARTY

NUMBER OF GUESTS

Menu

FOOD

WINE

_____

_____

_____

_____

_____

_____

_____

COST

_____

_____

_____

Guests

Comments

_____

_____

_____

_____

_____

_____

_____

_____

_____

_____

_____

_____

Occasion

DATE

TIME

PLACE

TYPE OF PARTY

NUMBER OF GUESTS

Menu

FOOD

WINE

COST

COST

Guests

Comments

_____

_____

_____

_____

_____

_____

_____

_____

_____

_____

_____

_____

_____

Occasion

DATE

TIME

PLACE

TYPE OF PARTY

NUMBER OF GUESTS

Menu

FOOD

WINE

COST

COST

Guests

Comments

_____

_____

_____

_____

_____

_____

_____

_____

_____

_____

_____

Occasion

DATE

TIME

PLACE

TYPE OF PARTY

NUMBER OF GUESTS

Menu

FOOD   WINE

COST   COST

Guests

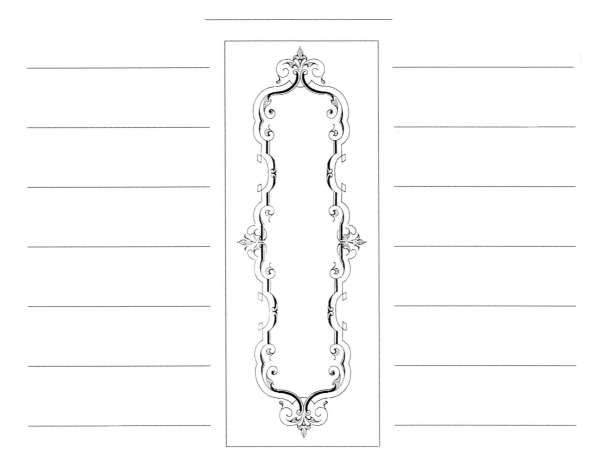

Comments

_____

_____

_____

_____

_____

_____

_____

_____

_____

_____

Occasion

DATE

TIME

PLACE

TYPE OF PARTY

NUMBER OF GUESTS

Menu

FOOD

WINE

COST

COST

Guests

Comments

_____

_____

_____

_____

_____

_____

_____

_____

_____

_____

Occasion

DATE

TIME

PLACE

TYPE OF PARTY

NUMBER OF GUESTS

Menu

FOOD   WINE

_____

_____

_____

_____

_____

_____

COST   COST

_____

_____

Guests

Comments

Occasion

DATE

TIME

PLACE

TYPE OF PARTY

NUMBER OF GUESTS

Menu

FOOD

WINE

COST

COST

Guests

_____

_____

_____

_____

_____

_____

_____

_____

_____

_____

_____

Guests

_____

_____

_____

_____

_____

_____

_____

_____

_____

_____

_____

Comments

Occasion

_____

DATE _____

TIME _____

PLACE _____

_____

_____

TYPE OF PARTY _____

_____

NUMBER OF GUESTS _____

_____

_____

Menu

FOOD

WINE

COST

COST

Guests

Guests

Comments

_____

_____

_____

_____

_____

_____

_____

_____

_____

_____

_____

_____

Occasion

DATE

TIME

PLACE

TYPE OF PARTY

NUMBER OF GUESTS

Menu

FOOD

_____   _____

_____   _____

_____   _____

_____   _____

_____   _____

_____   _____

_____   _____

COST

_____   _____

_____   _____

_____   _____

Menu

WINE

_____

_____

_____

_____

_____

_____

_____

COST

_____

_____

Guests

Guests

_____

_____

_____

_____

_____

_____

_____

_____

_____

_____

_____

Guests

Comments

Comments

_____

_____

_____

_____

_____

_____

_____

_____

_____

_____

Occasion

_____

DATE

TIME

PLACE

_____

_____

TYPE OF PARTY

_____

NUMBER OF GUESTS

_____

_____

Menu

FOOD

COST

Menu

WINE

COST

Guests

_____

_____

_____

_____

_____

_____

_____

_____

_____

_____

Guests

Guests

_____

_____

_____

_____

_____

_____

_____

_____

_____

_____

_____

Guests

_____

_____

_____

_____

_____

_____

_____

_____

_____

_____

Comments

Suppliers' Addresses

NAME _____

ADDRESS _____

_____

TELEPHONE _____

NAME _____

ADDRESS _____

_____

TELEPHONE _____

NAME _____

ADDRESS _____

_____

TELEPHONE _____

NAME _____

ADDRESS _____

_____

TELEPHONE _____

NAME _____

ADDRESS _____

_____

TELEPHONE _____

NAME _____

ADDRESS _____

_____

TELEPHONE _____

NAME _____

ADDRESS _____

_____

TELEPHONE _____

NAME _____

ADDRESS _____

_____

TELEPHONE _____

Suppliers' Addresses

NAME _____

ADDRESS _____

_____

TELEPHONE _____

NAME _____

ADDRESS _____

_____

TELEPHONE _____

NAME _____

ADDRESS _____

_____

TELEPHONE _____

NAME _____

ADDRESS _____

_____

TELEPHONE _____

NAME _____

ADDRESS _____

_____

TELEPHONE _____

NAME _____

ADDRESS _____

_____

TELEPHONE _____

NAME _____

ADDRESS _____

_____

TELEPHONE _____

NAME _____

ADDRESS _____

_____

TELEPHONE _____

Suppliers' Addresses

NAME _____

ADDRESS _____

_____

TELEPHONE _____

NAME _____

ADDRESS _____

_____

TELEPHONE _____

NAME _____

ADDRESS _____

_____

TELEPHONE _____

NAME _____

ADDRESS _____

_____

TELEPHONE _____

NAME _____

ADDRESS _____

_____

TELEPHONE _____

NAME _____

ADDRESS _____

_____

TELEPHONE _____

NAME _____

ADDRESS _____

_____

TELEPHONE _____

NAME _____

ADDRESS _____

_____

TELEPHONE _____

Suppliers' Addresses

NAME

ADDRESS

TELEPHONE

NAME

ADDRESS

TELEPHONE

NAME

ADDRESS

TELEPHONE

NAME

ADDRESS

TELEPHONE

NAME

ADDRESS

TELEPHONE

NAME

ADDRESS

TELEPHONE

NAME

ADDRESS

TELEPHONE

NAME

ADDRESS

TELEPHONE

Picture Credits

The Artist's Dinner Party: Viggo Johansen (1851-1935)
National Museum, Stockholm (The Bridgeman Art Library)

The Corner of the Table: Paul Chabas (1869-1937)
Musée des Beaux-Arts, Tourcoing (The Bridgeman Art Library)

Menu for the Mercers' Banquet (1859)
The Guildhall Library, London (The Bridgeman Art Library)

The Buffet: Jean Louis Forain (1852-1931)
Federation Mutualists Parisienne, Paris (Giraudon/The Bridgeman Art Library)

An Elegant Tea Party in the Artist's Studio: Madeleine Lemaire (1845-1928)
Fine Art Photographic Library Ltd

An Elegant Soirée in Summer: M. Snapes (19th/20th century)
Fine Art Photographic Library Ltd

An Elegant Soirée: Horace de Callas (d. 1921)
Fine Art Photographic Library Ltd

Souvenir d'un Soir: Joseph Marius Avy (1871-1939)
Musée de Routaix, France (The Bridgeman Art Library)

The Dinner Party: Sir Henry Cole (1808-82)
Philip Gale Fine Art, Chepstow (The Bridgeman Art Library)